began to go down, and Noah sent out a
bird to look for dry land. The bird came
back with a leaf from a tree.

At last Noah looked out and saw that
the water had all gone. He and his
family and all the animals came out
of the boat, and everyone thanked God
for keeping them alive.

God said, 'I will never again make a
flood like that. As long as the earth
lasts there will be seedtime and harvest.
And when it rains, I will put a rainbow
in the sky to let you know that I will
keep my word.'

Genesis 6–8

Abraham- the friend of God

'I want you to pack your things,' said God to Abraham one day, 'and go away from your home and all your friends. Take your family with you.'

Abraham said, 'Go where, Lord?'

'I will show you the way,' said God. 'You will be rich and all the people in the world will be happy because of you.'

Abraham trusted God, and he did what God said. He said goodbye to his friends and set off. After a long time Abraham came to the land of Canaan. 'This is it,' said God. 'Stop here.'

A Giraffe Book

God's special people

Stories from the Old Testament
retold by Margaret Ralph

Illustrated by Gordon King

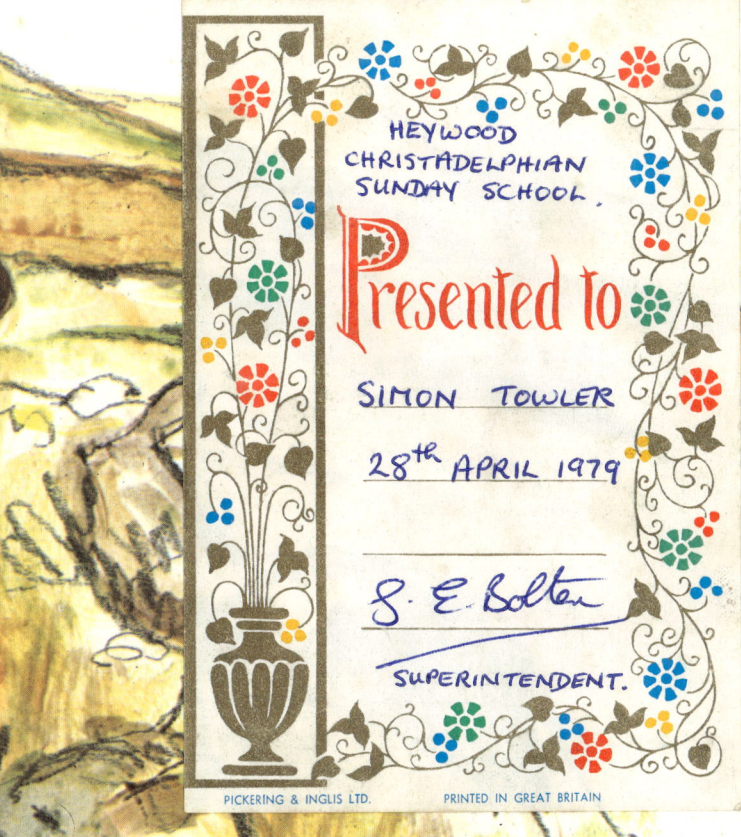

HEYWOOD
CHRISTADELPHIAN
SUNDAY SCHOOL.

Presented to

SIMON TOWLER

28th APRIL 1979

S. E. Bolten

SUPERINTENDENT.

PICKERING & INGLIS LTD.   PRINTED IN GREAT BRITAIN

Scripture Union/Purnell

Noah- the man God kept safe

'I want your money. I don't like you,' said one man to another. And he killed the man and took his money. All the men on the earth were like that. They were all bad. Only Noah loved God.

God said, 'These people are not fit to live on my earth. I will make a flood and let everyone die. But I will keep Noah and his family safe.'

So God said to Noah, 'Make a big boat, with three decks, a roof and a door.' And Noah did what God said. All the people made fun of Noah. They said, 'He's mad. Where's the water?' But Noah still did what God said.

Then God told Noah to put every kind of animal into the boat. And Noah did what God said. Last of all God told Noah and his family to go into the boat, and God shut the door.

The wind came. The rain began. It fell and fell for forty long days. Soon water hid all the land. But the boat sailed on the water, and Noah and his family were safe.

At last the rain stopped.

Then, after a long time, the water

Abraham and his wife, Sarah, were happy in their new home. But one thing made them sad. They were old, and they had no children.

'You will have a son,' said God to Abraham, and at last a baby was born. Abraham and Sarah called the baby Isaac, and they loved him very much.

A few years after this, God said to Abraham, 'Take Isaac to a hill which I will show you, and there kill him as an offering to me.'

Abraham could not understand this, but he still trusted God. Very sadly he went to the hill with Isaac. But just as Abraham was going to kill his son, God called out, 'Abraham, stop! Do not kill Isaac. Now I know that you trust me and that you will do everything I tell you to do.'

So God kept Isaac safe, and Abraham was very glad.

All his life Abraham trusted God, and we call him the friend of God.

Genesis 11–22

Jacob did not like his twin brother, Esau. Jacob said, 'It's not fair. Esau is only a little bit older than I am, yet Father is going to make him the next head of the family. Just because Esau likes hunting, and I don't, Father loves Esau best.'

Jacob kept on thinking about this, and it made him angry. Then, one day, Jacob and his mother played a trick on Esau.

Jacob's father, Isaac, was very old. Isaac called Esau and said, 'Hunt a deer, cook it, and bring it to me. Then I will make you the head of the family after me.'

Then Jacob's mother said to Jacob,

Jacob- the boy who ran away

'Quick. Kill two goats. I will cook them and you can take them to your father. He cannot see and he will think you are Esau.'

'But Father will know I am not Esau,' said Jacob. 'He will feel my smooth skin. Esau's skin is hairy.'

'Do as I say,' said his mother. 'I have a plan.'

So Jacob killed the goats. When he came back, his mother made him put on Esau's clothes, and she covered his hands with goat skin. She cooked the meat and Jacob took it to his father.

'Who are you?' asked Isaac.

'I am Esau,' said Jacob.

'You talk like Jacob,' said Isaac.

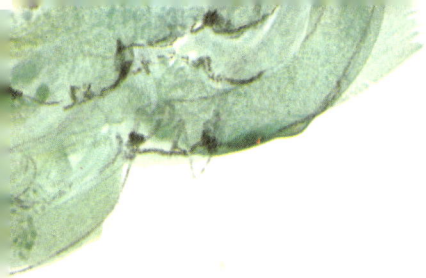

But Isaac felt the hairy goat skin on Jacob's arms, and he smelt the smell of Esau on the clothes. Isaac said, 'This must be Esau.' So he made Jacob the next head over the family.

Not long after, Esau came in, but he was too late.

Jacob looked at Esau's face and it was very angry. Jacob's mother said, 'Esau wants to kill you. You must go away.'

So Jacob ran away from home. He set out for his uncle's house, a long way off.

When night came he lay on the ground under the stars. It was dark and cold and lonely. For his pillow all he had was a stone.

That night he had a dream. He saw a ladder leading up to the sky, and angels were going up and down it. And God was there. God said, 'I will give you this land. I will be with you as you go away and I will bring you back.'

When Jacob woke up, he said, 'This is the gate to heaven. If God will help me, he shall be my God for ever.'

Then Jacob went on his way, and God was with him.

Genesis 27–28

Joseph- the boy with the beautiful coat

'I'm the best,' Joseph kept thinking. 'I'm much better than my ten older brothers.'

Joseph's father, Jacob, thought that Joseph was the best, too, and he gave Joseph a beautiful coat. He did not give the other brothers a coat like this.

One night Joseph dreamed that he and his brothers were cutting corn, and making it into bundles. Then all the bundles of corn bowed down to his bundle. He told the dream to his brothers. 'You are all going to bow down to me,' he said.

Joseph's brothers did not like him. 'He thinks he's better than us,' they said.

One day Joseph went to look for his brothers. He found them with the sheep, a long way from home. He looked at their faces, and saw that they were angry. They rushed at him, and grabbed him. 'Let's kill him,' they cried. They let him down into a pit.

But then they saw some men on camels on their way to Egypt. 'Now we can get rid of him without killing him,' the brothers said, 'and get some money, too. Let's sell him.'

So Joseph was led away to Egypt. He was very sad, and he began to pray to God.

In Egypt he was sold to a rich man. He worked well, and pleased his master. But the rich man's wife told lies about him, and he was put into prison. He still worked hard, and God was with him.

In prison he met the king's butler and baker. One night they had strange dreams. With God's help Joseph told them the meaning of the dreams. The dreams came true, and the butler was given his job back.

After two years Joseph was still in the prison. Then the king sent for him. He said to Joseph, 'I have had a dream and no one knows what it means. But the butler says you know the meaning of dreams.'

Joseph said, 'I don't, but God does.' So Joseph prayed. Then he said to the king, 'Your dream means that there will

be seven good years, when everything grows well, and then seven bad years, with no food.'

'What can we do?' asked the king.

'In the good years you must save the food,' said Joseph, 'and keep it for the bad years.'

'That's a good plan,' said the king. 'You shall see to it.'

So Joseph looked after all the food in Egypt. And when the bad years came there was plenty of food in Egypt, but in all the other lands people had no food.

One day Joseph saw some faces that he knew. Before him were his own brothers. They bowed low and begged for food. The dream that Joseph had when he was a boy was coming true. But his brothers did not know that this rich man was Joseph.

After some time Joseph said to them, 'I am your brother, Joseph.' He was so glad that he began to cry. But they were afraid. Joseph said, 'It's all right. God sent me here. Go home, bring my father, and I will look after you all.' So Joseph's father, and all his brothers, lived with Joseph in Egypt.

Genesis 37–47

Moses- the man who saved God's people

The great-great-great-great-grand-
children of Joseph all lived in
Egypt. One day the king of Egypt said,
'There are too many of these people
and soon they will take over my land.
We must make them work for us and
all their baby boys must be thrown into
the river.'

The people were very upset when the
king's men killed their babies. The
people said to God, 'God, you helped
Abraham. Please help us.'

One mother said, 'I will not let the
king kill my baby,' and she made a

plan. She put her baby in a little boat and placed the boat on the river.

The baby's sister hid near by. She saw the princess of Egypt come to wash in the river. She saw the princess find the baby, and smile at him.

She came to the princess. 'Shall I bring someone to look after him?' she asked. She fetched the baby's mother.

The princess said, 'This is Moses. Look after him for me. When he is older he shall live with me and be my son.'

So Moses went to live with the princess. But he didn't forget his people.

One day he saw an Egyptian beating one of them, and so he ran to help him. Then he was afraid of what the king would say. He ran far away and found a job looking after sheep.

A long time passed. One day, when
Moses was out with the sheep, he saw
a bush on fire. When he went to look
at it, God spoke to him. 'I have seen
how sad my people are,' said God, 'and
I am going to take them back to the
land of Canaan. You must go to the
king of Egypt and tell him to let the
people go.'

But Moses said, 'I can't do that. I
don't know how.'

'I will help you,' said God. So Moses
set off.

'You must let God's people go,' he told
the king.

But the king said, 'I won't do what your God says,' and he gave the people more work to do.

God made many bad things happen to the people of Egypt. But still the king would not let the people go.

Then the oldest child in every Egyptian house died and the king sent for Moses. 'Take your people away,' he said.

So Moses and the people left Egypt. But soon the king was sorry he had let them go. He sent his army to bring the people back.

Moses and the people came to the sea. Before them was the water. Behind them they saw the army. They were trapped. Then Moses prayed to God. And God sent a wind. All night long the wind blew the water away and the people crossed over on the dry sea bed. In the morning, when they were on the other side, the wind stopped and the water came back. The army could not get to the people. They were safe.

All the people thanked God and sang songs to him.

Exodus 1–15

Samuel- the boy who listened to God

Eli and his two sons looked after the temple of God. Eli loved God, but his sons did not. They did not do as God said.

One day Eli saw a lady, called Hannah, praying in the temple. Hannah was sad. 'Please let me have a baby,' she said to God. 'If I have a baby I will give him back to you, God, to work for you all his life.'

Some time later Hannah had a baby boy. She called him Samuel, and she loved him very much.

After a few years Hannah took Samuel to the temple to live with Eli. Samuel helped Eli in the temple. God was pleased, and Samuel and Hannah were very happy.

Late one night Samuel heard someone calling him. He ran to Eli.

'What do you want?' he said.

'I didn't call you,' said Eli. 'Go back to bed.'

Again Samuel heard someone call, and again he ran to Eli. 'You did call,' he said.

But still Eli said, 'It wasn't me.'

It was God who was speaking to Samuel. God called two more times and then Samuel said, 'Yes, Lord, I am listening.' So God talked to Samuel. Samuel had to tell Eli that God would punish his sons because they did not do as God said.

After that God often talked to Samuel and he became a leader of the people.

I Samuel 1–3

David- the boy
who looked afte

the sheep

David lived in Bethlehem with his father, Jesse, who was a farmer, and his seven older brothers. David's job was to look after the sheep when they were out on the hills. He loved God and God made him strong and brave.

One day his brother came running up the hill. 'David, come here,' he called.

'What do you want?' asked David.

'Samuel has come and he wants to see you,' said his brother.

'Samuel wants to see *me*? What for?' asked David.

'I don't know,' said his brother. 'Samuel came and asked to see all our father's sons. When he had looked at us all he said, "Are there any more?" Father told him that you were out with the sheep and Samuel said, "Go and bring him to me." You must go at once. I will look after the sheep.'

David ran down the hill, thinking of what his brother had said. What did Samuel want with him?

As soon as he got home his father took him to Samuel. When Samuel saw David, he looked happy. He said, 'David, God told me to come here. He has chosen you to be the next king of Israel.'

Samuel put some oil on David's head to show that he was to be made king. From that time on God was with David all the time.

I Samuel 16

Elijah-
the man who
trusted God

'Our God is Baal,' called the people.
'The God of Abraham is no good.'
When Elijah heard this he felt so sad
that he could have cried. 'The God of
Abraham is the true God,' he said.
'How can I let the people know this?'

He said to the king, 'God says he will
send no more rain until I ask him to.'
And there was no rain for three years.
But still the people did not pray to God
for help.

Then Elijah told the king, 'You must
bring all the people to the hill-top.
There Elijah talked to the people. 'You
men who trust Baal must make an
offering to him,' he said. So they made
a heap of stones and put a dead bull
on it.

'Now call out to Baal and ask him to
send down fire to burn your offering,'
said Elijah. All day long they called.
They danced round and round the
stones. But no fire came.

Then Elijah made a heap of stones,
and put a dead bull on it. He put water
all over it. He said, 'God, you are the
God of Abraham. Let all the people
know that you are the true God.'
There was a great flash. Fire came down
and burned up the bull.

Then the people said, 'Elijah's God
is the living God. We will do what he
says.'

That night rain fell again.

I Kings 17–18

Daniel- the mar

'The king has made a new law,' Daniel's
friends told him. 'The law says that
everyone must pray to the king and to
no other god. Anyone who does not
keep the law will be put into the den
of lions.'

'I will not pray to the king,' said
Daniel. 'I come from the land where we
pray to the true God, and I trust this
God.'

Then some men went to the king and
said, 'Daniel does not keep your law.
He is still praying to his God.'

This made the king very sad, because
he liked Daniel. All day long he tried
to think of a way to save Daniel, but

in the lions' den

there was no way.

At the end of the day he said to Daniel, 'Your God must look after you, for I cannot help you.' Then Daniel was put in the lions' den.

That night the king could not sleep. He kept thinking of the lions eating Daniel. In the morning he went to the lions' den. He called out, 'Daniel!'

'I am here,' said Daniel. 'My God has kept me safe.'

Then the king made a new law, saying, 'Everyone shall pray to Daniel's God. He is the living God.'

Daniel 6

Jonah- the man inside the fish

'I want you to go to Nineveh,' God said to a man named Jonah. 'The people there do many bad things which make me sad. Tell them that because of this I will punish them.'

'I don't want to,' said Jonah. And he ran away from God. He went to the sea and got on a ship going to a place far away from Nineveh.

Soon after the ship had left land God sent a strong wind so that the ship almost sank. The sailors called to their gods to help them, but still the storm went on. 'Get up and pray to your God,' they said to Jonah. 'See if he will help.'

'I pray to the living God who made the land and sea,' said Jonah. 'But I am running away from him.'

'Then this storm is because of you,' they said.

'Yes it is,' said Jonah. 'You must throw me into the sea.'

As they dropped him into the water, the storm stopped.

Just then God made a big fish swim by and it swallowed Jonah. It was dark and wet inside the fish. Jonah was in the fish for three days, and there he prayed to God. So God made the fish swim to land and spit up Jonah on the sand.

Then God told Jonah again to go to Nineveh.

This time Jonah went. He walked into the middle of Nineveh and called out to all the people. 'You have done many bad things,' he said, 'and God is angry with you.' He talked for a long time and then he left Nineveh. He sat down not far away to see what would happen.

When the king of Nineveh heard what Jonah had said he was sad. He told the people that they must stop doing these bad things and pray to God. And all the people did as he said.

God loved the people of Nineveh and when he saw they were sorry he gladly forgave them.

Jonah 1–3

Made and printed in Great Britain
by Purnell & Sons Ltd., Paulton.